D1473513

SORT YOUR $HIT OUT

A MONTHLY BUDGET PLANNER

A Monthly Budget Planner: Sort Your $hit Out!
by JAD Budget Planner Books

The font used on the copyright page of this book is FreeSans. This font is licensed as GPL (GNU General Public License) which permits a font to be used on the cover and interior of a commercially available physical book.

The font used on the cover, the page titles, and for the date numbers on the tracking pages is Roboto (copyright Christian Robertson). The font used for the monthly tabs is Roboto Bold (copyright Christian Robertson). The Roboto family of fonts is available under the Apache License v2.00 which permits the font to be used on the cover and interior of a commercially available physical book.

The emoticon images used at the end of each month are derived from a single image (copyright kanate). This image was purchased from Adobe Stock with a Standard License, which permits the image to be used in a product for resale providing the main value of the product is not the image itself.

The images used on the monthly title pages throughout this book are derived from a single image (copyright hvostik16). This image was purchased from Adobe Stock with a Standard License, which permits the image to be used in a product for resale providing the main value of the product is not the image itself.

The handwriting font used throughout this book is Segoe Print. A Desktop License for this font was purchased from Fonts.com. A Desktop License permits the use of a font on the cover and interior of commercially available physical books.

The images of notepad pages used throughout this book, are derived from a single image (copyright gmm2000) which was purchased from Adobe Stock with an Extended license. This license permits an image to be used on the cover and interior of a commercially available physical book where the image purchased forms a significant proportion of the value of the book.

Copyright © 2018 Dr Jason Davies
All rights reserved. No part of this publication may be reproduced, stored in a retrieval system, or transmitted in any form or by any means, electronic, mechanical, photocopying, recording or otherwise, without the prior written permission of the publisher.

ISBN: 9781981062836

```
****************************************
8/06/18          TIME  9:36:39PM
-7086338881      5429298042138665

       Sine  Irish Pub
1327 E. CARY & 14TH STREETS
    RICHMOND, VIRGINIA
         23219
      (804) 549-7761
 you for visiting Sine Irish pub!
 us online at www.sineirishpub.com

TRD XXXXXXXXXX3244      S
002555    CORNER CPL CHECK    3066
JTH            BAR      AA BAR 3


                    41.00
                     5.25
    --------------------------
JBTOTAL  $      46.25
    TIP  $........10.75.
 TOTAL   $........57.75.
    ----------------------------
              57.75
 CUSTOMER  COPY
****************************************
```

Disclaimer: All information found in this book, including any ideas, opinions, views, predictions, forecasts, commentaries, or suggestions, expressed or implied herein, are for informational, entertainment or educational purposes only and should not be construed as personal or financial advice. While the information provided is believed to be accurate, it may include errors or inaccuracies. In no event shall the author and/or publisher be liable, whether in contract, tort (including negligence) or otherwise, in respect of any damage, expense or other loss you may suffer arising out of such information or any reliance you may place upon such information. Conduct your own due diligence, or consult a licensed financial adviser or broker before making any and all financial decisions. Any decisions made or actions taken on the basis of any information found in this book, expressed or implied herein, are committed at your own risk, financial or otherwise. In no event shall the author and/or publisher be liable for any damages whatsoever arising out of the use of or inability to use this book.

You don't have to start this budget planner in January. If you start in a different month, then simply return to January at the end of the year to continue.

January

Create a Monthly Budget

****** MONEY COMING IN ******

Income 1	$
Income 2	$
Other income	$

TOTAL INCOME $ _____

****** MONEY GOING OUT ******

HOUSING

Mortgage or Rent	$
Real Estate Taxes	$
Maintenance/Repairs	$
Insurance	$

UTILITIES

Electricity	$
Water	$
Gas/Oil	$
Sewer	$
Trash	$
Cable/Satellite	$
Internet	$
Phone/Cell Phones	$

ANIMALS/PETS

Veterinary Costs	$
Food/Miscellaneous	$

FAMILY

Groceries	$
Child Care/Sitter	$
Toiletries	$
Hair Care	$
School/College Fees	$
School Supplies	$
Maintenance Payments	$
Subscriptions	$
Organizational Dues	$
Children's Allowances	$

HOUSEHOLD

Decorating/Furnishing	$
Garden	$
House Cleaning	$
Household Items	$
Laundry/Dry Cleaning	$

HEALTH

Life Insurance	$
Health Insurance	$
Dental Insurance	$
Doctor Visits	$
Dentist	$
Optometrist	$
Medicine	$

TRANSPORTATION

Car Payment/s	$
Fuel	$
Maintenance/Repair	$
Insurance	$
Travel Fares/Tickets	$

CLOTHING

Adult/s	$
Children	$

CELEBRATIONS

Birthday/s	$
Christmas/Holidays	$

RECREATION

Entertainment	$
Dining Out	$
Socializing	$
Vacation	$

DEBTS

Credit Card #1	$
Credit Card #2	$
Credit Card #3	$
Credit Card #4	$
Other Debts	$

SAVINGS

Emergency Fund	$
Retirement Fund	$
College Fund	$
Pension Contributions	$

OTHER OUTGOINGS

	$
	$

TOTAL OUTGOINGS $ _____

**** BUDGET CALCULATION ****

TOTAL INCOME	$ _____
- TOTAL OUTGOINGS	$ _____
	$ _____

If your total outgoings are greater than your total income, then you could find yourself getting further and further into debt. If this is the case, then it is important that you address the situation. You can do this by **REDUCING YOUR NON-ESSENTIAL SPENDING** and/or **INCREASING YOUR INCOME.**

Track Your Daily Spending

circle the day

M T W Th F S Su 1st

Description	Amount

Daily Total:

M T W Th F S Su 2nd

Description	Amount

Daily Total:

M T W Th F S Su 3rd

Description	Amount

Daily Total:

M T W Th F S Su 4th

Description	Amount

Daily Total:

M T W Th F S Su   5th

Description	Amount
Daily Total:	

M T W Th F S Su   6th

Description	Amount
Daily Total:	

M T W Th F S Su   7th

Description	Amount
Daily Total:	

M T W Th F S Su   8th

Description	Amount
Daily Total:	

So far this month, I have spent: $

Track Your Daily Spending

circle the day

M T W Th F S Su 9th

Description	Amount
Daily Total:	

M T W Th F S Su 10th

Description	Amount
Daily Total:	

M T W Th F S Su 11th

Description	Amount
Daily Total:	

M T W Th F S Su 12th

Description	Amount
Daily Total:	

M T W Th F S Su 13th

Description	Amount
Daily Total:	

M T W Th F S Su 14th

Description	Amount
Daily Total:	

M T W Th F S Su 15th

Description	Amount
Daily Total:	

M T W Th F S Su 16th

Description	Amount
Daily Total:	

So far this month, I have spent: $

Track Your Daily Spending

circle the day

M T W Th F S Su **17**th

Description	Amount
Daily Total:	

M T W Th F S Su **18**th

Description	Amount
Daily Total:	

M T W Th F S Su **19**th

Description	Amount
Daily Total:	

M T W Th F S Su **20**th

Description	Amount
Daily Total:	

M T W Th F S Su 21st

Description	Amount
Daily Total:	

M T W Th F S Su 22nd

Description	Amount
Daily Total:	

M T W Th F S Su 23rd

Description	Amount
Daily Total:	

M T W Th F S Su 24th

Description	Amount
Daily Total:	

So far this month, I have spent: $

Track Your Daily Spending

circle the day →

M T W Th F S Su	25th
Description	Amount
Daily Total:	

M T W Th F S Su	26th
Description	Amount
Daily Total:	

M T W Th F S Su	27th
Description	Amount
Daily Total:	

M T W Th F S Su	28th
Description	Amount
Daily Total:	

M T W Th F S Su 29th

Description	Amount
Daily Total:	

M T W Th F S Su 30th

Description	Amount
Daily Total:	

M T W Th F S Su 31st

Description	Amount
Daily Total:	

** MONTHLY BUDGET CHECK **

MONTHLY INCOME $
- TOTAL SPEND $ _____
                     $ _____

How do you feel about your spending this month?

☹ ☹ 😐 😀 😄

☐ ☐ ☐ ☐ ☐

I overspent   I was sensible!

What have you learned by tracking your spending this month? Write down your thoughts over the page.

WRITE DOWN YOUR THOUGHTS ABOUT THIS MONTH'S SPENDING

For example, you could ask yourself: Am I living within my means? Am I happier with my spending this month compared to last month? How can I cut down on non-essential spending? How can I increase my income? Can I afford a few treats? What lessons have I learned this month that I can put into practice next month?

February

Create a Monthly Budget

****** MONEY COMING IN ******

Income 1	$
Income 2	$
Other income	$
TOTAL INCOME	$ _____

****** MONEY GOING OUT ******

HOUSING

Mortgage or Rent	$
Real Estate Taxes	$
Maintenance/Repairs	$
Insurance	$

UTILITIES

Electricity	$
Water	$
Gas/Oil	$
Sewer	$
Trash	$
Cable/Satellite	$
Internet	$
Phone/Cell Phones	$

ANIMALS/PETS

Veterinary Costs	$
Food/Miscellaneous	$

FAMILY

Groceries	$
Child Care/Sitter	$
Toiletries	$
Hair Care	$
School/College Fees	$
School Supplies	$
Maintenance Payments	$
Subscriptions	$
Organizational Dues	$
Children's Allowances	$

HOUSEHOLD

Decorating/Furnishing	$
Garden	$
House Cleaning	$
Household Items	$
Laundry/Dry Cleaning	$

HEALTH

Life Insurance	$
Health Insurance	$
Dental Insurance	$
Doctor Visits	$
Dentist	$
Optometrist	$
Medicine	$

TRANSPORTATION

Car Payment/s	$
Fuel	$
Maintenance/Repair	$
Insurance	$
Travel Fares/Tickets	$

CLOTHING

Adult/s	$
Children	$

CELEBRATIONS

Birthday/s	$
Christmas/Holidays	$

RECREATION

Entertainment	$
Dining Out	$
Socializing	$
Vacation	$

DEBTS

Credit Card #1	$
Credit Card #2	$
Credit Card #3	$
Credit Card #4	$
Other Debts	$

SAVINGS

Emergency Fund	$
Retirement Fund	$
College Fund	$
Pension Contributions	$

OTHER OUTGOINGS

	$
	$

TOTAL OUTGOINGS $ _____

**** BUDGET CALCULATION ****

TOTAL INCOME	$
- TOTAL OUTGOINGS	$ _____
	$ _____

If your total outgoings are greater than your total income, then you could find yourself getting further and further into debt. If this is the case, then it is important that you address the situation. You can do this by REDUCING YOUR NON-ESSENTIAL SPENDING and/or INCREASING YOUR INCOME.

Track Your Daily Spending

circle the day →

| M T W Th F S Su | **1**st |
Description	Amount

Daily Total:

| M T W Th F S Su | **2**nd |
Description	Amount

Daily Total:

| M T W Th F S Su | **3**rd |
Description	Amount

Daily Total:

| M T W Th F S Su | **4**th |
Description	Amount

Daily Total:

M T W Th F S Su   5th

Description	Amount
Daily Total:	

M T W Th F S Su   6th

Description	Amount
Daily Total:	

M T W Th F S Su   7th

Description	Amount
Daily Total:	

M T W Th F S Su   8th

Description	Amount
Daily Total:	

So far this month, I have spent: $

Track Your Daily Spending

circle the day

M T W Th F S Su **9**th

Description	Amount
Daily Total:	

M T W Th F S Su **10**th

Description	Amount
Daily Total:	

M T W Th F S Su **11**th

Description	Amount
Daily Total:	

M T W Th F S Su **12**th

Description	Amount
Daily Total:	

M T W Th F S Su 13th

Description	Amount
Daily Total:	

M T W Th F S Su 14th

Description	Amount
Daily Total:	

M T W Th F S Su 15th

Description	Amount
Daily Total:	

M T W Th F S Su 16th

Description	Amount
Daily Total:	

So far this month, I have spent: $

Track Your Daily Spending

circle the day

M T W Th F S Su	**17**th
Description	Amount
Daily Total:	

M T W Th F S Su	**18**th
Description	Amount
Daily Total:	

M T W Th F S Su	**19**th
Description	Amount
Daily Total:	

M T W Th F S Su	**20**th
Description	Amount
Daily Total:	

M T W Th F S Su 21st

Description	Amount
Daily Total:	

M T W Th F S Su 22nd

Description	Amount
Daily Total:	

M T W Th F S Su 23rd

Description	Amount
Daily Total:	

M T W Th F S Su 24th

Description	Amount
Daily Total:	

So far this month, I have spent: $

Track Your Daily Spending

circle the day

M T W Th F S Su 25th

Description	Amount
Daily Total:	

M T W Th F S Su 26th

Description	Amount
Daily Total:	

M T W Th F S Su 27th

Description	Amount
Daily Total:	

M T W Th F S Su 28th

Description	Amount
Daily Total:	

M T W Th F S Su **29**th

Description	Amount

Daily Total:

← Only fill this in if
it is a leap year.

** MONTHLY BUDGET CHECK **

MONTHLY INCOME $
– TOTAL SPEND $ _____
                              $ _____

How do you feel about your spending
this month?

☹ 🙁 😐 🙂 😄

☐ ☐ ☐ ☐ ☐

I overspent   I was sensible!

What have you learned by tracking your spending this
month? Write down your thoughts over the page.

WRITE DOWN YOUR THOUGHTS ABOUT THIS MONTH'S SPENDING

For example, you could ask yourself: Am I living within my means? Am I happier with my spending this month compared to last month? How can I cut down on non-essential spending? How can I increase my income? Can I afford a few treats? What lessons have I learned this month that I can put into practice next month?

March

Create a Monthly Budget

****** MONEY COMING IN ******

Income 1 $

Income 2 $

Other income $

TOTAL INCOME $ _____

****** MONEY GOING OUT ******

HOUSING

Mortgage or Rent $

Real Estate Taxes $

Maintenance/Repairs $

Insurance $

UTILITIES

Electricity $

Water $

Gas/Oil $

Sewer $

Trash $

Cable/Satellite $

Internet $

Phone/Cell Phones $

ANIMALS/PETS

Veterinary Costs $

Food/Miscellaneous $

FAMILY

Groceries $

Child Care/Sitter $

Toiletries $

Hair Care $

School/College Fees $

School Supplies $

Maintenance Payments $

Subscriptions $

Organizational Dues $

Children's Allowances $

HOUSEHOLD

Decorating/Furnishing $

Garden $

House Cleaning $

Household Items $

Laundry/Dry Cleaning $

HEALTH

Life Insurance $

Health Insurance $

Dental Insurance $

Doctor Visits $

Dentist $

Optometrist $

Medicine $

TRANSPORTATION

Car Payment/s	$
Fuel	$
Maintenance/Repair	$
Insurance	$
Travel Fares/Tickets	$

CLOTHING

Adult/s	$
Children	$

CELEBRATIONS

Birthday/s	$
Christmas/Holidays	$

RECREATION

Entertainment	$
Dining Out	$
Socializing	$
Vacation	$

DEBTS

Credit Card #1	$
Credit Card #2	$
Credit Card #3	$
Credit Card #4	$
Other Debts	$

SAVINGS

Emergency Fund	$
Retirement Fund	$
College Fund	$
Pension Contributions	$

OTHER OUTGOINGS

	$
	$

TOTAL OUTGOINGS $ _____

**** BUDGET CALCULATION ****

TOTAL INCOME	$ _____
- TOTAL OUTGOINGS	$ _____
	$ _____

If your total outgoings are greater than your total income, then you could find yourself getting further and further into debt. If this is the case, then it is important that you address the situation. You can do this by **REDUCING YOUR NON-ESSENTIAL SPENDING** and/or **INCREASING YOUR INCOME.**

Track Your Daily Spending

circle the day

M T W Th F S Su	1st
Description	Amount
Daily Total:	

M T W Th F S Su	2nd
Description	Amount
Daily Total:	

M T W Th F S Su	3rd
Description	Amount
Daily Total:	

M T W Th F S Su	4th
Description	Amount
Daily Total:	

M T W Th F S Su — 5th

Description	Amount

Daily Total:

M T W Th F S Su — 6th

Description	Amount

Daily Total:

M T W Th F S Su — 7th

Description	Amount

Daily Total:

M T W Th F S Su — 8th

Description	Amount

Daily Total:

So far this month, I have spent: $

Track Your Daily Spending

circle the day

M T W Th F S Su — 9th

Description	Amount
Daily Total:	

M T W Th F S Su — 10th

Description	Amount
Daily Total:	

M T W Th F S Su — 11th

Description	Amount
Daily Total:	

M T W Th F S Su — 12th

Description	Amount
Daily Total:	

M T W Th F S Su 13th

Description	Amount
Daily Total:	

M T W Th F S Su 14th

Description	Amount
Daily Total:	

M T W Th F S Su 15th

Description	Amount
Daily Total:	

M T W Th F S Su 16th

Description	Amount
Daily Total:	

So far this month, I have spent: $

Track Your Daily Spending

circle the day

M T W Th F S Su **17**th

Description	Amount
Daily Total:	

M T W Th F S Su **18**th

Description	Amount
Daily Total:	

M T W Th F S Su **19**th

Description	Amount
Daily Total:	

M T W Th F S Su **20**th

Description	Amount
Daily Total:	

M T W Th F S Su 21st

Description	Amount
Daily Total:	

M T W Th F S Su 22nd

Description	Amount
Daily Total:	

M T W Th F S Su 23rd

Description	Amount
Daily Total:	

M T W Th F S Su 24th

Description	Amount
Daily Total:	

So far this month, I have spent: $

Track Your Daily Spending

circle the day

M T W Th F S Su 25th

Description	Amount
Daily Total:	

M T W Th F S Su 26th

Description	Amount
Daily Total:	

M T W Th F S Su 27th

Description	Amount
Daily Total:	

M T W Th F S Su 28th

Description	Amount
Daily Total:	

M T W Th F S Su 29th

Description	Amount
Daily Total:	

M T W Th F S Su 30th

Description	Amount
Daily Total:	

M T W Th F S Su 31st

Description	Amount
Daily Total:	

** MONTHLY BUDGET CHECK **

MONTHLY INCOME $

- TOTAL SPEND $

$

How do you feel about your spending this month?

☹ ☹ 😐 😀 😄

☐ ☐ ☐ ☐ ☐

I overspent   I was sensible!

What have you learned by tracking your spending this month? Write down your thoughts over the page.

WRITE DOWN YOUR THOUGHTS ABOUT THIS MONTH'S SPENDING

For example, you could ask yourself: Am I living within my means? Am I happier with my spending this month compared to last month? How can I cut down on non-essential spending? How can I increase my income? Can I afford a few treats? What lessons have I learned this month that I can put into practice next month?

April

APR

Create a Monthly Budget

****** MONEY COMING IN ******

Income 1	$
Income 2	$
Other income	$

TOTAL INCOME $ _____

****** MONEY GOING OUT ******

HOUSING

Mortgage or Rent	$
Real Estate Taxes	$
Maintenance/Repairs	$
Insurance	$

UTILITIES

Electricity	$
Water	$
Gas/Oil	$
Sewer	$
Trash	$
Cable/Satellite	$
Internet	$
Phone/Cell Phones	$

ANIMALS/PETS

Veterinary Costs	$
Food/Miscellaneous	$

FAMILY

Groceries	$
Child Care/Sitter	$
Toiletries	$
Hair Care	$
School/College Fees	$
School Supplies	$
Maintenance Payments	$
Subscriptions	$
Organizational Dues	$
Children's Allowances	$

HOUSEHOLD

Decorating/Furnishing	$
Garden	$
House Cleaning	$
Household Items	$
Laundry/Dry Cleaning	$

HEALTH

Life Insurance	$
Health Insurance	$
Dental Insurance	$
Doctor Visits	$
Dentist	$
Optometrist	$
Medicine	$

TRANSPORTATION

Car Payment/s $
Fuel $
Maintenance/Repair $
Insurance $
Travel Fares/Tickets $

CLOTHING

Adult/s $
Children $

CELEBRATIONS

Birthday/s $
Christmas/Holidays $

RECREATION

Entertainment $
Dining Out $
Socializing $
Vacation $

DEBTS

Credit Card #1 $
Credit Card #2 $
Credit Card #3 $
Credit Card #4 $
Other Debts $

SAVINGS

Emergency Fund $
Retirement Fund $
College Fund $
Pension Contributions $

OTHER OUTGOINGS

     $
     $

TOTAL OUTGOINGS $ _____

**** BUDGET CALCULATION ****

TOTAL INCOME $
- TOTAL OUTGOINGS $ _____
     $ _____

If your total outgoings are greater than your total income, then you could find yourself getting further and further into debt. If this is the case, then it is important that you address the situation. You can do this by **REDUCING YOUR NON-ESSENTIAL SPENDING** and/or **INCREASING YOUR INCOME.**

Track Your Daily Spending

circle the day

M T W Th F S Su	1st
Description	Amount
Daily Total:	

M T W Th F S Su	2nd
Description	Amount
Daily Total:	

M T W Th F S Su	3rd
Description	Amount
Daily Total:	

M T W Th F S Su	4th
Description	Amount
Daily Total:	

M T W Th F S Su — 5th

Description	Amount
Daily Total:	

M T W Th F S Su — 6th

Description	Amount
Daily Total:	

M T W Th F S Su — 7th

Description	Amount
Daily Total:	

M T W Th F S Su — 8th

Description	Amount
Daily Total:	

So far this month, I have spent: $

Track Your Daily Spending

circle the day

M T W Th F S Su **9**th

Description	Amount
Daily Total:	

M T W Th F S Su **10**th

Description	Amount
Daily Total:	

M T W Th F S Su **11**th

Description	Amount
Daily Total:	

M T W Th F S Su **12**th

Description	Amount
Daily Total:	

M T W Th F S Su 13th

Description	Amount
Daily Total:	

M T W Th F S Su 14th

Description	Amount
Daily Total:	

M T W Th F S Su 15th

Description	Amount
Daily Total:	

M T W Th F S Su 16th

Description	Amount
Daily Total:	

So far this month, I have spent: $

Track Your Daily Spending

circle the day

| M T W Th F S Su | 17th |
Description	Amount
Daily Total:	

| M T W Th F S Su | 18th |
Description	Amount
Daily Total:	

| M T W Th F S Su | 19th |
Description	Amount
Daily Total:	

| M T W Th F S Su | 20th |
Description	Amount
Daily Total:	

M T W Th F S Su **21**st

Description	Amount
Daily Total:	

M T W Th F S Su **22**nd

Description	Amount
Daily Total:	

M T W Th F S Su **23**rd

Description	Amount
Daily Total:	

M T W Th F S Su **24**th

Description	Amount
Daily Total:	

So far this month, I have spent: $

Track Your Daily Spending

circle the day

M T W Th F S Su 25th

Description	Amount
Daily Total:	

M T W Th F S Su 26th

Description	Amount
Daily Total:	

M T W Th F S Su 27th

Description	Amount
Daily Total:	

M T W Th F S Su 28th

Description	Amount
Daily Total:	

M T W Th F S Su 29th

Description	Amount

Daily Total:

M T W Th F S Su 30th

Description	Amount

Daily Total:

** MONTHLY BUDGET CHECK **

MONTHLY INCOME $

– TOTAL SPEND $ _____

$ _____

How do you feel about your spending this month?

☹ ☹ 😐 🙂 😄

☐ ☐ ☐ ☐ ☐

I overspent   I was sensible!

What have you learned by tracking your spending this month? Write down your thoughts over the page.

WRITE DOWN YOUR THOUGHTS ABOUT THIS MONTH'S SPENDING

For example, you could ask yourself: Am I living within my means? Am I happier with my spending this month compared to last month? How can I cut down on non-essential spending? How can I increase my income? Can I afford a few treats? What lessons have I learned this month that I can put into practice next month?

May

Create a Monthly Budget

****** MONEY COMING IN ******

Income 1 $
Income 2 $
Other income $

TOTAL INCOME $ _____

****** MONEY GOING OUT ******

HOUSING

Mortgage or Rent $
Real Estate Taxes $
Maintenance/Repairs $
Insurance $

UTILITIES

Electricity $
Water $
Gas/Oil $
Sewer $
Trash $
Cable/Satellite $
Internet $
Phone/Cell Phones $

ANIMALS/PETS

Veterinary Costs $
Food/Miscellaneous $

FAMILY

Groceries $
Child Care/Sitter $
Toiletries $
Hair Care $
School/College Fees $
School Supplies $
Maintenance Payments $
Subscriptions $
Organizational Dues $
Children's Allowances $

HOUSEHOLD

Decorating/Furnishing $
Garden $
House Cleaning $
Household Items $
Laundry/Dry Cleaning $

HEALTH

Life Insurance $
Health Insurance $
Dental Insurance $
Doctor Visits $
Dentist $
Optometrist $
Medicine $

TRANSPORTATION

Car Payment/s	$
Fuel	$
Maintenance/Repair	$
Insurance	$
Travel Fares/Tickets	$

CLOTHING

Adult/s	$
Children	$

CELEBRATIONS

Birthday/s	$
Christmas/Holidays	$

RECREATION

Entertainment	$
Dining Out	$
Socializing	$
Vacation	$

DEBTS

Credit Card #1	$
Credit Card #2	$
Credit Card #3	$
Credit Card #4	$
Other Debts	$

SAVINGS

Emergency Fund	$
Retirement Fund	$
College Fund	$
Pension Contributions	$

OTHER OUTGOINGS

	$
	$

TOTAL OUTGOINGS $ _____

____ BUDGET CALCULATION ____

TOTAL INCOME	$
− TOTAL OUTGOINGS	$ _____
	$ _____

If your total outgoings are greater than your total income, then you could find yourself getting further and further into debt. If this is the case, then it is important that you address the situation. You can do this by **REDUCING YOUR NON-ESSENTIAL SPENDING** and/or **INCREASING YOUR INCOME.**

Track Your Daily Spending

circle the day

M T W Th F S Su 1st

Description	Amount
Daily Total:	

M T W Th F S Su 2nd

Description	Amount
Daily Total:	

M T W Th F S Su 3rd

Description	Amount
Daily Total:	

M T W Th F S Su 4th

Description	Amount
Daily Total:	

M T W Th F S Su — 5th

Description	Amount
Daily Total:	

M T W Th F S Su — 6th

Description	Amount
Daily Total:	

M T W Th F S Su — 7th

Description	Amount
Daily Total:	

M T W Th F S Su — 8th

Description	Amount
Daily Total:	

So far this month, I have spent: $

Track Your Daily Spending

circle the day

M T W Th F S Su **9**th

Description	Amount
Daily Total:	

M T W Th F S Su **10**th

Description	Amount
Daily Total:	

M T W Th F S Su **11**th

Description	Amount
Daily Total:	

M T W Th F S Su **12**th

Description	Amount
Daily Total:	

M T W Th F S Su 13th

Description	Amount
Daily Total:	

M T W Th F S Su 14th

Description	Amount
Daily Total:	

M T W Th F S Su 15th

Description	Amount
Daily Total:	

M T W Th F S Su 16th

Description	Amount
Daily Total:	

So far this month, I have spent: $

Track Your Daily Spending

circle the day

M T W Th F S Su 17th

Description	Amount
Daily Total:	

M T W Th F S Su 18th

Description	Amount
Daily Total:	

M T W Th F S Su 19th

Description	Amount
Daily Total:	

M T W Th F S Su 20th

Description	Amount
Daily Total:	

M T W Th F S Su **21**st

Description	Amount
Daily Total:	

M T W Th F S Su **22**nd

Description	Amount
Daily Total:	

M T W Th F S Su **23**rd

Description	Amount
Daily Total:	

M T W Th F S Su **24**th

Description	Amount
Daily Total:	

MAY

So far this month, I have spent: $

Track Your Daily Spending

circle the day

M T W Th F S Su 25th

Description	Amount
Daily Total:	

M T W Th F S Su 26th

Description	Amount
Daily Total:	

M T W Th F S Su 27th

Description	Amount
Daily Total:	

M T W Th F S Su 28th

Description	Amount
Daily Total:	

M T W Th F S Su 29th

Description	Amount
Daily Total:	

M T W Th F S Su 30th

Description	Amount
Daily Total:	

M T W Th F S Su 31st

Description	Amount
Daily Total:	

** MONTHLY BUDGET CHECK **

MONTHLY INCOME $

- TOTAL SPEND $ _____

$ _____

How do you feel about your spending this month?

☹ ☹ 😐 🙂 😄

☐ ☐ ☐ ☐ ☐

I overspent   I was sensible!

What have you learned by tracking your spending this month? Write down your thoughts over the page.

WRITE DOWN YOUR THOUGHTS ABOUT THIS MONTH'S SPENDING

For example, you could ask yourself: Am I living within my means? Am I happier with my spending this month compared to last month? How can I cut down on non-essential spending? How can I increase my income? Can I afford a few treats? What lessons have I learned this month that I can put into practice next month?

June

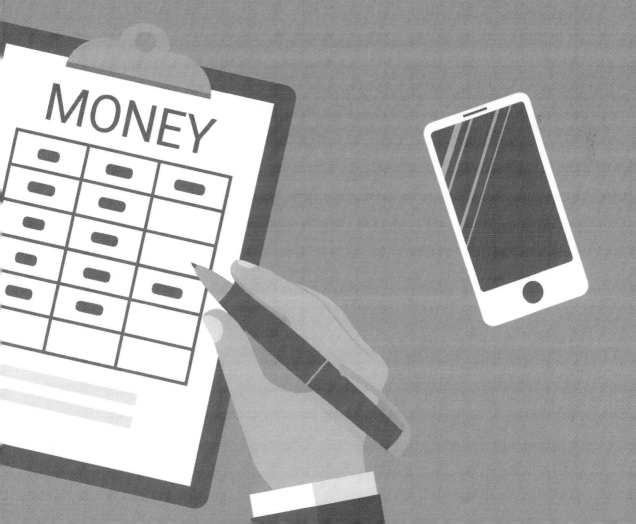

Create a Monthly Budget

****** MONEY COMING IN ******

Income 1 $
Income 2 $
Other income $

TOTAL INCOME $ _____

****** MONEY GOING OUT ******

HOUSING

Mortgage or Rent $
Real Estate Taxes $
Maintenance/Repairs $
Insurance $

UTILITIES

Electricity $
Water $
Gas/Oil $
Sewer $
Trash $
Cable/Satellite $
Internet $
Phone/Cell Phones $

ANIMALS/PETS

Veterinary Costs $
Food/Miscellaneous $

FAMILY

Groceries $
Child Care/Sitter $
Toiletries $
Hair Care $
School/College Fees $
School Supplies $
Maintenance Payments $
Subscriptions $
Organizational Dues $
Children's Allowances $

HOUSEHOLD

Decorating/Furnishing $
Garden $
House Cleaning $
Household Items $
Laundry/Dry Cleaning $

HEALTH

Life Insurance $
Health Insurance $
Dental Insurance $
Doctor Visits $
Dentist $
Optometrist $
Medicine $

TRANSPORTATION

Car Payment/s	$
Fuel	$
Maintenance/Repair	$
Insurance	$
Travel Fares/Tickets	$

CLOTHING

Adult/s	$
Children	$

CELEBRATIONS

Birthday/s	$
Christmas/Holidays	$

RECREATION

Entertainment	$
Dining Out	$
Socializing	$
Vacation	$

DEBTS

Credit Card #1	$
Credit Card #2	$
Credit Card #3	$
Credit Card #4	$
Other Debts	$

SAVINGS

Emergency Fund	$
Retirement Fund	$
College Fund	$
Pension Contributions	$

OTHER OUTGOINGS

	$
	$
TOTAL OUTGOINGS	$ _____

**** BUDGET CALCULATION ****

TOTAL INCOME	$
- TOTAL OUTGOINGS	$ _____
	$ _____

If your total outgoings are greater than your total income, then you could find yourself getting further and further into debt. If this is the case, then it is important that you address the situation. You can do this by REDUCING YOUR NON-ESSENTIAL SPENDING and/or INCREASING YOUR INCOME.

Track Your Daily Spending

circle the day

M T W Th F S Su   1st

Description	Amount
Daily Total:	

M T W Th F S Su   2nd

Description	Amount
Daily Total:	

M T W Th F S Su   3rd

Description	Amount
Daily Total:	

M T W Th F S Su   4th

Description	Amount
Daily Total:	

M T W Th F S Su **5**th

Description	Amount
Daily Total:	

M T W Th F S Su **6**th

Description	Amount
Daily Total:	

M T W Th F S Su **7**th

Description	Amount
Daily Total:	

M T W Th F S Su **8**th

Description	Amount
Daily Total:	

JUN

So far this month, I have spent: **$**

Track Your Daily Spending

circle the day

M T W Th F S Su	**9**th
Description	Amount
Daily Total:	

M T W Th F S Su	**10**th
Description	Amount
Daily Total:	

M T W Th F S Su	**11**th
Description	Amount
Daily Total:	

M T W Th F S Su	**12**th
Description	Amount
Daily Total:	

M T W Th F S Su 13th

Description	Amount
Daily Total:	

M T W Th F S Su 14th

Description	Amount
Daily Total:	

M T W Th F S Su 15th

Description	Amount
Daily Total:	

M T W Th F S Su 16th

Description	Amount
Daily Total:	

So far this month, I have spent: $

Track Your Daily Spending

circle the day

M T W Th F S Su 17th

Description	Amount
Daily Total:	

M T W Th F S Su 18th

Description	Amount
Daily Total:	

M T W Th F S Su 19th

Description	Amount
Daily Total:	

M T W Th F S Su 20th

Description	Amount
Daily Total:	

M T W Th F S Su 21st

Description	Amount
Daily Total:	

M T W Th F S Su 22nd

Description	Amount
Daily Total:	

M T W Th F S Su 23rd

Description	Amount
Daily Total:	

M T W Th F S Su 24th

Description	Amount
Daily Total:	

JUN

So far this month, I have spent: $

Track Your Daily Spending

circle the day

| M T W Th F S Su 25th |
Description	Amount
Daily Total:	

| M T W Th F S Su 26th |
Description	Amount
Daily Total:	

| M T W Th F S Su 27th |
Description	Amount
Daily Total:	

| M T W Th F S Su 28th |
Description	Amount
Daily Total:	

M T W Th F S Su 29th

Description	Amount
Daily Total:	

M T W Th F S Su 30th

Description	Amount
Daily Total:	

** MONTHLY BUDGET CHECK **

MONTHLY INCOME $

− TOTAL SPEND $ _____

$ _____

How do you feel about your spending this month?

☐ ☐ ☐ ☐ ☐

I overspent   I was sensible!

What have you learned by tracking your spending this month? Write down your thoughts over the page.

WRITE DOWN YOUR THOUGHTS ABOUT THIS MONTH'S SPENDING

For example, you could ask yourself: Am I living within my means? Am I happier with my spending this month compared to last month? How can I cut down on non-essential spending? How can I increase my income? Can I afford a few treats? What lessons have I learned this month that I can put into practice next month?

July

JUL

Create a Monthly Budget

****** MONEY COMING IN ******

Income 1 $

Income 2 $

Other income $

TOTAL INCOME $ _____

****** MONEY GOING OUT ******

HOUSING

Mortgage or Rent $

Real Estate Taxes $

Maintenance/Repairs $

Insurance $

UTILITIES

Electricity $

Water $

Gas/Oil $

Sewer $

Trash $

Cable/Satellite $

Internet $

Phone/Cell Phones $

ANIMALS/PETS

Veterinary Costs $

Food/Miscellaneous $

FAMILY

Groceries $

Child Care/Sitter $

Toiletries $

Hair Care $

School/College Fees $

School Supplies $

Maintenance Payments $

Subscriptions $

Organizational Dues $

Children's Allowances $

HOUSEHOLD

Decorating/Furnishing $

Garden $

House Cleaning $

Household Items $

Laundry/Dry Cleaning $

HEALTH

Life Insurance $

Health Insurance $

Dental Insurance $

Doctor Visits $

Dentist $

Optometrist $

Medicine $

TRANSPORTATION

Car Payment/s	$
Fuel	$
Maintenance/Repair	$
Insurance	$
Travel Fares/Tickets	$

CLOTHING

Adult/s	$
Children	$

CELEBRATIONS

Birthday/s	$
Christmas/Holidays	$

RECREATION

Entertainment	$
Dining Out	$
Socializing	$
Vacation	$

DEBTS

Credit Card #1	$
Credit Card #2	$
Credit Card #3	$
Credit Card #4	$
Other Debts	$

SAVINGS

Emergency Fund	$
Retirement Fund	$
College Fund	$
Pension Contributions	$

OTHER OUTGOINGS

	$
	$

TOTAL OUTGOINGS	$

**** BUDGET CALCULATION ****

TOTAL INCOME	$
- TOTAL OUTGOINGS	$
	$

If your total outgoings are greater than your total income, then you could find yourself getting further and further into debt. If this is the case, then it is important that you address the situation. You can do this by REDUCING YOUR NON-ESSENTIAL SPENDING and/or INCREASING YOUR INCOME.

Track Your Daily Spending

circle the day

M T W Th F S Su — 1st

Description	Amount

Daily Total:

M T W Th F S Su — 2nd

Description	Amount

Daily Total:

M T W Th F S Su — 3rd

Description	Amount

Daily Total:

M T W Th F S Su — 4th

Description	Amount

Daily Total:

M T W Th F S Su **5**th

Description	Amount
Daily Total:	

M T W Th F S Su **6**th

Description	Amount
Daily Total:	

M T W Th F S Su **7**th

Description	Amount
Daily Total:	

M T W Th F S Su **8**th

Description	Amount
Daily Total:	

So far this month, I have spent: **$**

Track Your Daily Spending

circle the day

M T W Th F S Su **9**th

Description	Amount

Daily Total:

M T W Th F S Su **10**th

Description	Amount

Daily Total:

M T W Th F S Su **11**th

Description	Amount

Daily Total:

M T W Th F S Su **12**th

Description	Amount

Daily Total:

M T W Th F S Su 13th

Description	Amount
Daily Total:	

M T W Th F S Su 14th

Description	Amount
Daily Total:	

M T W Th F S Su 15th

Description	Amount
Daily Total:	

M T W Th F S Su 16th

Description	Amount
Daily Total:	

JUL

So far this month, I have spent: $

Track Your Daily Spending

circle the day

M T W Th F S Su 17th

Description	Amount
Daily Total:	

M T W Th F S Su 18th

Description	Amount
Daily Total:	

M T W Th F S Su 19th

Description	Amount
Daily Total:	

M T W Th F S Su 20th

Description	Amount
Daily Total:	

M T W Th F S Su **21**st

Description	Amount
Daily Total:	

M T W Th F S Su **22**nd

Description	Amount
Daily Total:	

M T W Th F S Su **23**rd

Description	Amount
Daily Total:	

M T W Th F S Su **24**th

Description	Amount
Daily Total:	

JUL

So far this month, I have spent: **$**

Track Your Daily Spending

circle the day

M T W Th F S Su 25th

Description	Amount
Daily Total:	

M T W Th F S Su 26th

Description	Amount
Daily Total:	

M T W Th F S Su 27th

Description	Amount
Daily Total:	

M T W Th F S Su 28th

Description	Amount
Daily Total:	

M T W Th F S Su 29th

Description	Amount
Daily Total:	

M T W Th F S Su 30th

Description	Amount
Daily Total:	

M T W Th F S Su 31st

Description	Amount
Daily Total:	

** MONTHLY BUDGET CHECK **

MONTHLY INCOME $ _____
- TOTAL SPEND $ _____
                  $ _____

How do you feel about your spending this month?

☹ 🙁 😐 🙂 😄

☐ ☐ ☐ ☐ ☐

I overspent   I was sensible!

What have you learned by tracking your spending this month? Write down your thoughts over the page.

WRITE DOWN YOUR THOUGHTS ABOUT THIS MONTH'S SPENDING

For example, you could ask yourself: Am I living within my means? Am I happier with my spending this month compared to last month? How can I cut down on non-essential spending? How can I increase my income? Can I afford a few treats? What lessons have I learned this month that I can put into practice next month?

August

AUG

Create a Monthly Budget

****** MONEY COMING IN ******

Income 1	$ 3,012.31
Income 2	$
Other income	$

TOTAL INCOME $ 3,012.31

****** MONEY GOING OUT ******

HOUSING

Mortgage or Rent	$ 1,351.95
Real Estate Taxes	$
Maintenance/Repairs	$
Insurance	$ 103.40

UTILITIES

Electricity	$
Water	$
Gas/Oil	$
Sewer	$
Trash	$
Cable/Satellite	$
Internet	$
Phone/Cell Phones	$ —

ANIMALS/PETS

Veterinary Costs	$
Food/Miscellaneous	$

FAMILY

Groceries	$
Child Care/Sitter	$
Toiletries	$
Hair Care	$
School/College Fees	$
School Supplies	$
Maintenance Payments	$
Subscriptions	$
Organizational Dues	$
Children's Allowances	$

HOUSEHOLD

Decorating/Furnishing	$
Garden	$
House Cleaning	$
Household Items	$
Laundry/Dry Cleaning	$

HEALTH

Life Insurance	$
Health Insurance	$
Dental Insurance	$
Doctor Visits	$
Dentist	$
Optometrist	$
Medicine	$

TRANSPORTATION

Car Payment/s	$
Fuel	$
Maintenance/Repair	$
Insurance	$
Travel Fares/Tickets	$

CLOTHING

Adult/s	$
Children	$

CELEBRATIONS

Birthday/s	$
Christmas/Holidays	$

RECREATION

Entertainment	$
Dining Out	$
Socializing	$
Vacation	$

DEBTS

Credit Card #1	$
Credit Card #2	$
Credit Card #3	$
Credit Card #4	$
Other Debts	$

SAVINGS

Emergency Fund	$
Retirement Fund	$
College Fund	$
Pension Contributions	$

OTHER OUTGOINGS

	$
	$

TOTAL OUTGOINGS	$

**** BUDGET CALCULATION ****

TOTAL INCOME	$
- TOTAL OUTGOINGS	$
	$

If your total outgoings are greater than your total income, then you could find yourself getting further and further into debt. If this is the case, then it is important that you address the situation. You can do this by REDUCING YOUR NON-ESSENTIAL SPENDING and/or INCREASING YOUR INCOME.

AUG

Track Your Daily Spending

circle the day

M T (W) Th F S Su — 1st

Description	Amount
Horace Mann	103.40
Rent	1,351.95

Daily Total:

M T W Th F S Su — 2nd

Description	Amount

Daily Total:

M T W Th F S Su — 3rd

Description	Amount

Daily Total:

M T W Th F S Su — 4th

Description	Amount

Daily Total:

M T W Th F S Su **5**th

Description	Amount
Daily Total:	

M T W Th F S Su **6**th

Description	Amount
Daily Total:	

M T W Th F S Su **7**th

Description	Amount
Daily Total:	

M T W Th F S Su **8**th

Description	Amount
Daily Total:	

AUG

So far this month, I have spent: **$**

Track Your Daily Spending

circle the day

M T W Th F S Su 9th

Description	Amount

Daily Total:

M T W Th F S Su 10th

Description	Amount

Daily Total:

M T W Th F S Su 11th

Description	Amount

Daily Total:

M T W Th F S Su 12th

Description	Amount

Daily Total:

M T W Th F S Su **13**th

Description	Amount

Daily Total:

M T W Th F S Su **14**th

Description	Amount

Daily Total:

M T W Th F S Su **15**th

Description	Amount

Daily Total:

M T W Th F S Su **16**th

Description	Amount

Daily Total:

AUG

So far this month, I have spent: $

Track Your Daily Spending

circle the day

M T W Th F S Su **17**th

Description	Amount
Daily Total:	

M T W Th F S Su **18**th

Description	Amount
Daily Total:	

M T W Th F S Su **19**th

Description	Amount
Daily Total:	

M T W Th F S Su **20**th

Description	Amount
Daily Total:	

M T W Th F S Su 21st

Description	Amount
Daily Total:	

M T W Th F S Su 22nd

Description	Amount
Daily Total:	

M T W Th F S Su 23rd

Description	Amount
Daily Total:	

M T W Th F S Su 24th

Description	Amount
Daily Total:	

AUG

So far this month, I have spent: $

Track Your Daily Spending

M T W Th F S Su **25**th

circle the day

Description	Amount
Daily Total:	

M T W Th F S Su **26**th

Description	Amount
Daily Total:	

M T W Th F S Su **27**th

Description	Amount
Daily Total:	

M T W Th F S Su **28**th

Description	Amount
Daily Total:	

M T W Th F S Su 29th

Description	Amount
Daily Total:	

M T W Th F S Su 30th

Description	Amount
Daily Total:	

M T W Th F S Su 31st

Description	Amount
Daily Total:	

** MONTHLY BUDGET CHECK **

MONTHLY INCOME $

- TOTAL SPEND $
_____
$

How do you feel about your spending this month?

☹ ☹ 😐 🙂 😄

☐ ☐ ☐ ☐ ☐

I overspent   I was sensible!

What have you learned by tracking your spending this month? Write down your thoughts over the page.

WRITE DOWN YOUR THOUGHTS ABOUT THIS MONTH'S SPENDING

For example, you could ask yourself: Am I living within my means? Am I happier with my spending this month compared to last month? How can I cut down on non-essential spending? How can I increase my income? Can I afford a few treats? What lessons have I learned this month that I can put into practice next month?

September

SEP

Create a Monthly Budget

****** MONEY COMING IN ******

Income 1	$
Income 2	$
Other income	$
TOTAL INCOME	$

****** MONEY GOING OUT ******

HOUSING

Mortgage or Rent	$
Real Estate Taxes	$
Maintenance/Repairs	$
Insurance	$

UTILITIES

Electricity	$
Water	$
Gas/Oil	$
Sewer	$
Trash	$
Cable/Satellite	$
Internet	$
Phone/Cell Phones	$

ANIMALS/PETS

Veterinary Costs	$
Food/Miscellaneous	$

FAMILY

Groceries	$
Child Care/Sitter	$
Toiletries	$
Hair Care	$
School/College Fees	$
School Supplies	$
Maintenance Payments	$
Subscriptions	$
Organizational Dues	$
Children's Allowances	$

HOUSEHOLD

Decorating/Furnishing	$
Garden	$
House Cleaning	$
Household Items	$
Laundry/Dry Cleaning	$

HEALTH

Life Insurance	$
Health Insurance	$
Dental Insurance	$
Doctor Visits	$
Dentist	$
Optometrist	$
Medicine	$

TRANSPORTATION

Car Payment/s $

Fuel $

Maintenance/Repair $

Insurance $

Travel Fares/Tickets $

CLOTHING

Adult/s $

Children $

CELEBRATIONS

Birthday/s $

Christmas/Holidays $

RECREATION

Entertainment $

Dining Out $

Socializing $

Vacation $

DEBTS

Credit Card #1 $

Credit Card #2 $

Credit Card #3 $

Credit Card #4 $

Other Debts $

SAVINGS

Emergency Fund $

Retirement Fund $

College Fund $

Pension Contributions $

OTHER OUTGOINGS

     $

     $

TOTAL OUTGOINGS $ _____

**** BUDGET CALCULATION ****

     TOTAL INCOME $

     - TOTAL OUTGOINGS $ _____

     $ _____

If your total outgoings are greater than your total income, then you could find yourself getting further and further into debt. If this is the case, then it is important that you address the situation. You can do this by **REDUCING YOUR NON-ESSENTIAL SPENDING** and/or **INCREASING YOUR INCOME.**

Track Your Daily Spending

circle the day

M T W Th F S Su — 1st

Description	Amount
Daily Total:	

M T W Th F S Su — 2nd

Description	Amount
Daily Total:	

M T W Th F S Su — 3rd

Description	Amount
Daily Total:	

M T W Th F S Su — 4th

Description	Amount
Daily Total:	

M T W Th F S Su **5**th

Description	Amount
Daily Total:	

M T W Th F S Su **6**th

Description	Amount
Daily Total:	

M T W Th F S Su **7**th

Description	Amount
Daily Total:	

M T W Th F S Su **8**th

Description	Amount
Daily Total:	

SEP

So far this month, I have spent: **$**

Track Your Daily Spending

circle the day

M T W Th F S Su **9**th

Description	Amount
Daily Total:	

M T W Th F S Su **10**th

Description	Amount
Daily Total:	

M T W Th F S Su **11**th

Description	Amount
Daily Total:	

M T W Th F S Su **12**th

Description	Amount
Daily Total:	

M T W Th F S Su 13th

Description	Amount
Daily Total:	

M T W Th F S Su 14th

Description	Amount
Daily Total:	

M T W Th F S Su 15th

Description	Amount
Daily Total:	

M T W Th F S Su 16th

Description	Amount
Daily Total:	

So far this month, I have spent: $

Track Your Daily Spending

circle the day

M T W Th F S Su — 17th

Description	Amount
Daily Total:	

M T W Th F S Su — 18th

Description	Amount
Daily Total:	

M T W Th F S Su — 19th

Description	Amount
Daily Total:	

M T W Th F S Su — 20th

Description	Amount
Daily Total:	

M T W Th F S Su **21**st

Description	Amount
Daily Total:	

M T W Th F S Su **22**nd

Description	Amount
Daily Total:	

M T W Th F S Su **23**rd

Description	Amount
Daily Total:	

M T W Th F S Su **24**th

Description	Amount
Daily Total:	

So far this month, I have spent: **$**

Track Your Daily Spending

circle the day

M T W Th F S Su	25th
Description	Amount
Daily Total:	

M T W Th F S Su	26th
Description	Amount
Daily Total:	

M T W Th F S Su	27th
Description	Amount
Daily Total:	

M T W Th F S Su	28th
Description	Amount
Daily Total:	

M T W Th F S Su 29th

Description	Amount

Daily Total:

M T W Th F S Su 30th

Description	Amount

Daily Total:

** MONTHLY BUDGET CHECK **

MONTHLY INCOME $

– TOTAL SPEND $ _____

$ _____

How do you feel about your spending this month?

I overspent   I was sensible!

What have you learned by tracking your spending this month? Write down your thoughts over the page.

WRITE DOWN YOUR THOUGHTS ABOUT THIS MONTH'S SPENDING

For example, you could ask yourself: Am I living within my means? Am I happier with my spending this month compared to last month? How can I cut down on non-essential spending? How can I increase my income? Can I afford a few treats? What lessons have I learned this month that I can put into practice next month?

October

OCT

Create a Monthly Budget

****** **MONEY COMING IN** ******

Income 1 $
Income 2 $
Other income $

TOTAL INCOME $ _____

****** **MONEY GOING OUT** ******

HOUSING

Mortgage or Rent $
Real Estate Taxes $
Maintenance/Repairs $
Insurance $

UTILITIES

Electricity $
Water $
Gas/Oil $
Sewer $
Trash $
Cable/Satellite $
Internet $
Phone/Cell Phones $

ANIMALS/PETS

Veterinary Costs $
Food/Miscellaneous $

FAMILY

Groceries $
Child Care/Sitter $
Toiletries $
Hair Care $
School/College Fees $
School Supplies $
Maintenance Payments $
Subscriptions $
Organizational Dues $
Children's Allowances $

HOUSEHOLD

Decorating/Furnishing $
Garden $
House Cleaning $
Household Items $
Laundry/Dry Cleaning $

HEALTH

Life Insurance $
Health Insurance $
Dental Insurance $
Doctor Visits $
Dentist $
Optometrist $
Medicine $

TRANSPORTATION

Car Payment/s $ _____
Fuel $ _____
Maintenance/Repair $ _____
Insurance $ _____
Travel Fares/Tickets $ _____

CLOTHING

Adult/s $ _____
Children $ _____

CELEBRATIONS

Birthday/s $ _____
Christmas/Holidays $ _____

RECREATION

Entertainment $ _____
Dining Out $ _____
Socializing $ _____
Vacation $ _____

DEBTS

Credit Card #1 $ _____
Credit Card #2 $ _____
Credit Card #3 $ _____
Credit Card #4 $ _____
Other Debts $ _____

SAVINGS

Emergency Fund $ _____
Retirement Fund $ _____
College Fund $ _____
Pension Contributions $ _____

OTHER OUTGOINGS

_____ $ _____
_____ $ _____

TOTAL OUTGOINGS $ _____

**** **BUDGET CALCULATION** ****

TOTAL INCOME $ _____
- TOTAL OUTGOINGS $ _____
                        $ _____

If your total outgoings are greater than your total income, then you could find yourself getting further and further into debt. If this is the case, then it is important that you address the situation. You can do this by **REDUCING YOUR NON-ESSENTIAL SPENDING** and/or **INCREASING YOUR INCOME.**

Track Your Daily Spending

circle the day

M T W Th F S Su   1st

Description	Amount
Daily Total:	

M T W Th F S Su   2nd

Description	Amount
Daily Total:	

M T W Th F S Su   3rd

Description	Amount
Daily Total:	

M T W Th F S Su   4th

Description	Amount
Daily Total:	

M T W Th F S Su	5th
Description	Amount
Daily Total:	

M T W Th F S Su	6th
Description	Amount
Daily Total:	

M T W Th F S Su	7th
Description	Amount
Daily Total:	

M T W Th F S Su	8th
Description	Amount
Daily Total:	

So far this month, I have spent: $ _____

Track Your Daily Spending

circle the day

M T W Th F S Su — 9th

Description	Amount
Daily Total:	

M T W Th F S Su — 10th

Description	Amount
Daily Total:	

M T W Th F S Su — 11th

Description	Amount
Daily Total:	

M T W Th F S Su — 12th

Description	Amount
Daily Total:	

M T W Th F S Su 13th

Description	Amount
Daily Total:	

M T W Th F S Su 14th

Description	Amount
Daily Total:	

M T W Th F S Su 15th

Description	Amount
Daily Total:	

M T W Th F S Su 16th

Description	Amount
Daily Total:	

OCT

So far this month, I have spent: $

Track Your Daily Spending

circle the day

M T W Th F S Su **17**th

Description	Amount
Daily Total:	

M T W Th F S Su **18**th

Description	Amount
Daily Total:	

M T W Th F S Su **19**th

Description	Amount
Daily Total:	

M T W Th F S Su **20**th

Description	Amount
Daily Total:	

M T W Th F S Su **21**st

Description	Amount
Daily Total:	

M T W Th F S Su **22**nd

Description	Amount
Daily Total:	

M T W Th F S Su **23**rd

Description	Amount
Daily Total:	

M T W Th F S Su **24**th

Description	Amount
Daily Total:	

OCT

So far this month, I have spent: **$**

Track Your Daily Spending

circle the day

M T W Th F S Su **25**th

Description	Amount
Daily Total:	

M T W Th F S Su **26**th

Description	Amount
Daily Total:	

M T W Th F S Su **27**th

Description	Amount
Daily Total:	

M T W Th F S Su **28**th

Description	Amount
Daily Total:	

M T W Th F S Su 29th

Description	Amount

Daily Total:

M T W Th F S Su 30th

Description	Amount

Daily Total:

M T W Th F S Su 31st

Description	Amount

Daily Total:

** MONTHLY BUDGET CHECK **

MONTHLY INCOME $

− TOTAL SPEND $ _____

$ _____

How do you feel about your spending this month?

☐ ☐ ☐ ☐ ☐

I overspent   I was sensible!

What have you learned by tracking your spending this month? Write down your thoughts over the page.

WRITE DOWN YOUR THOUGHTS ABOUT THIS MONTH'S SPENDING

For example, you could ask yourself: Am I living within my means? Am I happier with my spending this month compared to last month? How can I cut down on non-essential spending? How can I increase my income? Can I afford a few treats? What lessons have I learned this month that I can put into practice next month?

November

NOV

Create a Monthly Budget

****** MONEY COMING IN ******

Income 1 $
Income 2 $
Other income $

TOTAL INCOME $ _____

****** MONEY GOING OUT ******

HOUSING

Mortgage or Rent $
Real Estate Taxes $
Maintenance/Repairs $
Insurance $

UTILITIES

Electricity $
Water $
Gas/Oil $
Sewer $
Trash $
Cable/Satellite $
Internet $
Phone/Cell Phones $

ANIMALS/PETS

Veterinary Costs $
Food/Miscellaneous $

FAMILY

Groceries $
Child Care/Sitter $
Toiletries $
Hair Care $
School/College Fees $
School Supplies $
Maintenance Payments $
Subscriptions $
Organizational Dues $
Children's Allowances $

HOUSEHOLD

Decorating/Furnishing $
Garden $
House Cleaning $
Household Items $
Laundry/Dry Cleaning $

HEALTH

Life Insurance $
Health Insurance $
Dental Insurance $
Doctor Visits $
Dentist $
Optometrist $
Medicine $

TRANSPORTATION

Car Payment/s $

Fuel $

Maintenance/Repair $

Insurance $

Travel Fares/Tickets $

CLOTHING

Adult/s $

Children $

CELEBRATIONS

Birthday/s $

Christmas/Holidays $

RECREATION

Entertainment $

Dining Out $

Socializing $

Vacation $

DEBTS

Credit Card #1 $

Credit Card #2 $

Credit Card #3 $

Credit Card #4 $

Other Debts $

SAVINGS

Emergency Fund $

Retirement Fund $

College Fund $

Pension Contributions $

OTHER OUTGOINGS

$

$

TOTAL OUTGOINGS $ _____

**** BUDGET CALCULATION ****

TOTAL INCOME $

- TOTAL OUTGOINGS $ _____

$ _____

If your total outgoings are greater than your total income, then you could find yourself getting further and further into debt. If this is the case, then it is important that you address the situation. You can do this by **REDUCING YOUR NON-ESSENTIAL SPENDING** and/or **INCREASING YOUR INCOME.**

Track Your Daily Spending

circle the day

M T W Th F S Su 1st

Description	Amount
Daily Total:	

M T W Th F S Su 2nd

Description	Amount
Daily Total:	

M T W Th F S Su 3rd

Description	Amount
Daily Total:	

M T W Th F S Su 4th

Description	Amount
Daily Total:	

M T W Th F S Su 5th

Description	Amount
Daily Total:	

M T W Th F S Su 6th

Description	Amount
Daily Total:	

M T W Th F S Su 7th

Description	Amount
Daily Total:	

M T W Th F S Su 8th

Description	Amount
Daily Total:	

NOV

So far this month, I have spent: $

Track Your Daily Spending

circle the day

M T W Th F S Su **9**th

Description	Amount
Daily Total:	

M T W Th F S Su **10**th

Description	Amount
Daily Total:	

M T W Th F S Su **11**th

Description	Amount
Daily Total:	

M T W Th F S Su **12**th

Description	Amount
Daily Total:	

M T W Th F S Su 13th

Description	Amount
Daily Total:	

M T W Th F S Su 14th

Description	Amount
Daily Total:	

M T W Th F S Su 15th

Description	Amount
Daily Total:	

M T W Th F S Su 16th

Description	Amount
Daily Total:	

NOV

So far this month, I have spent: $

Track Your Daily Spending

circle the day

M T W Th F S Su **17**th

Description	Amount

Daily Total:

M T W Th F S Su **18**th

Description	Amount

Daily Total:

M T W Th F S Su **19**th

Description	Amount

Daily Total:

M T W Th F S Su **20**th

Description	Amount

Daily Total:

M T W Th F S Su **21**st

Description	Amount
Daily Total:	

M T W Th F S Su **22**nd

Description	Amount
Daily Total:	

M T W Th F S Su **23**rd

Description	Amount
Daily Total:	

M T W Th F S Su **24**th

Description	Amount
Daily Total:	

NOV

So far this month, I have spent: **$**

Track Your Daily Spending

circle the day

M T W Th F S Su **25**th

Description	Amount
Daily Total:	

M T W Th F S Su **26**th

Description	Amount
Daily Total:	

M T W Th F S Su **27**th

Description	Amount
Daily Total:	

M T W Th F S Su **28**th

Description	Amount
Daily Total:	

M T W Th F S Su **29**th

Description	Amount
Daily Total:	

M T W Th F S Su **30**th

Description	Amount
Daily Total:	

** MONTHLY BUDGET CHECK **

MONTHLY INCOME $

− TOTAL SPEND $

$

How do you feel about your spending this month?

☹ ☹ 😐 🙂 😄

☐ ☐ ☐ ☐ ☐

I overspent   I was sensible!

What have you learned by tracking your spending this month? Write down your thoughts over the page.

WRITE DOWN YOUR THOUGHTS ABOUT THIS MONTH'S SPENDING

For example, you could ask yourself: Am I living within my means? Am I happier with my spending this month compared to last month? How can I cut down on non-essential spending? How can I increase my income? Can I afford a few treats? What lessons have I learned this month that I can put into practice next month?

December

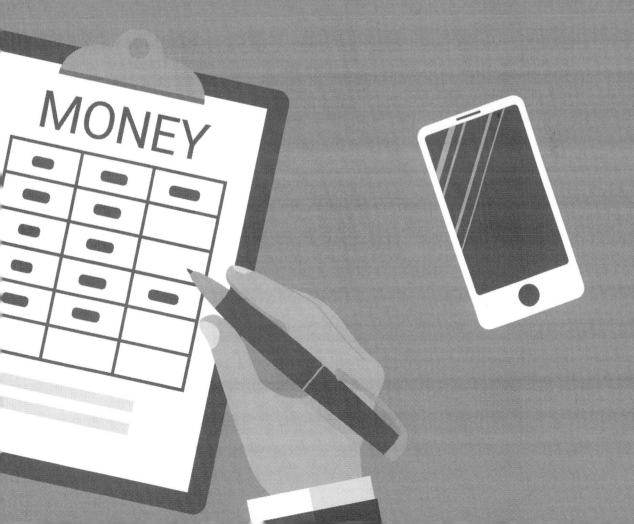

Create a Monthly Budget

****** MONEY COMING IN ******

Income 1 $
Income 2 $
Other income $

TOTAL INCOME $

****** MONEY GOING OUT ******

HOUSING

Mortgage or Rent $
Real Estate Taxes $
Maintenance/Repairs $
Insurance $

UTILITIES

Electricity $
Water $
Gas/Oil $
Sewer $
Trash $
Cable/Satellite $
Internet $
Phone/Cell Phones $

ANIMALS/PETS

Veterinary Costs $
Food/Miscellaneous $

FAMILY

Groceries $
Child Care/Sitter $
Toiletries $
Hair Care $
School/College Fees $
School Supplies $
Maintenance Payments $
Subscriptions $
Organizational Dues $
Children's Allowances $

HOUSEHOLD

Decorating/Furnishing $
Garden $
House Cleaning $
Household Items $
Laundry/Dry Cleaning $

HEALTH

Life Insurance $
Health Insurance $
Dental Insurance $
Doctor Visits $
Dentist $
Optometrist $
Medicine $

TRANSPORTATION

Car Payment/s	$
Fuel	$
Maintenance/Repair	$
Insurance	$
Travel Fares/Tickets	$

CLOTHING

Adult/s	$
Children	$

CELEBRATIONS

Birthday/s	$
Christmas/Holidays	$

RECREATION

Entertainment	$
Dining Out	$
Socializing	$
Vacation	$

DEBTS

Credit Card #1	$
Credit Card #2	$
Credit Card #3	$
Credit Card #4	$
Other Debts	$

SAVINGS

Emergency Fund	$
Retirement Fund	$
College Fund	$
Pension Contributions	$

OTHER OUTGOINGS

	$
	$

TOTAL OUTGOINGS $ _____

**** BUDGET CALCULATION ****

TOTAL INCOME	$
- TOTAL OUTGOINGS	$ _____
	$ _____

If your total outgoings are greater than your total income, then you could find yourself getting further and further into debt. If this is the case, then it is important that you address the situation. You can do this by **REDUCING YOUR NON-ESSENTIAL SPENDING** and/or **INCREASING YOUR INCOME.**

DEC

Track Your Daily Spending

circle the day

M T W Th F S Su   **1**st

Description	Amount
Daily Total:	

M T W Th F S Su   **2**nd

Description	Amount
Daily Total:	

M T W Th F S Su   **3**rd

Description	Amount
Daily Total:	

M T W Th F S Su   **4**th

Description	Amount
Daily Total:	

M T W Th F S Su 5th

Description	Amount
Daily Total:	

M T W Th F S Su 6th

Description	Amount
Daily Total:	

M T W Th F S Su 7th

Description	Amount
Daily Total:	

M T W Th F S Su 8th

Description	Amount
Daily Total:	

So far this month, I have spent:

DEC

Track Your Daily Spending

circle the day

M T W Th F S Su **9**th

Description	Amount

Daily Total:

M T W Th F S Su **10**th

Description	Amount

Daily Total:

M T W Th F S Su **11**th

Description	Amount

Daily Total:

M T W Th F S Su **12**th

Description	Amount

Daily Total:

M T W Th F S Su 13th

Description	Amount
Daily Total:	

M T W Th F S Su 14th

Description	Amount
Daily Total:	

M T W Th F S Su 15th

Description	Amount
Daily Total:	

M T W Th F S Su 16th

Description	Amount
Daily Total:	

So far this month, I have spent: $

DEC

Track Your Daily Spending

circle the day

M T W Th F S Su **17**th

Description	Amount
Daily Total:	

M T W Th F S Su **18**th

Description	Amount
Daily Total:	

M T W Th F S Su **19**th

Description	Amount
Daily Total:	

M T W Th F S Su **20**th

Description	Amount
Daily Total:	

M T W Th F S Su 21st

Description	Amount
Daily Total:	

M T W Th F S Su 22nd

Description	Amount
Daily Total:	

M T W Th F S Su 23rd

Description	Amount
Daily Total:	

M T W Th F S Su 24th

Description	Amount
Daily Total:	

So far this month, I have spent: **$**

DEC

Track Your Daily Spending

circle the day

M T W Th F S Su 25th

Description	Amount

Daily Total:

M T W Th F S Su 26th

Description	Amount

Daily Total:

M T W Th F S Su 27th

Description	Amount

Daily Total:

M T W Th F S Su 28th

Description	Amount

Daily Total:

M T W Th F S Su 29th

Description	Amount
Daily Total:	

M T W Th F S Su 30th

Description	Amount
Daily Total:	

M T W Th F S Su 31st

Description	Amount
Daily Total:	

** MONTHLY BUDGET CHECK **

MONTHLY INCOME $

− TOTAL SPEND $

$

How do you feel about your spending this month?

☐　☐　☐　☐　☐

I overspent   I was sensible!

What have you learned by tracking your spending this month? Write down your thoughts over the page.

WRITE DOWN YOUR THOUGHTS ABOUT THIS MONTH'S SPENDING

For example, you could ask yourself: Am I living within my means? Am I happier with my spending this month compared to last month? How can I cut down on non-essential spending? How can I increase my income? Can I afford a few treats? What lessons have I learned this month that I can put into practice next month?

79343170R10084

Made in the USA
Middletown, DE
10 July 2018